CLIMBING THE LADDER TO LEADERSHIP
DR. CLAYTON D. BERRY

Copyright: 2018
All Rights Reserved
Printed in the United States of America
ISBN-13: 978-0-9890167-4-2
ISBN-10: 0-9890167-4-9

All scriptural reference derived from the King James Version of the Holy Bible.

All copies are prohibited without the express written consent of the author.

BOOK DR. CLAYTON D. BERRY FOR YOUR NEXT CONFERENCE, WORKSHOP OR SEMINAR
SEND YOUR REQUEST TO CLAYTONDBERRY@AOL.COM

THIS WORKBOOK IS DEDICATED TO MY LATE GRANDMOTHER MOTHER LEE HESTER EDWARDS. JANUARY 13, 1925 - FEBRUARY 13, 2018.

TABLE OF CONTENTS

LEADERSHIP EXPLORATION............PG. 5
LESSON 1..PG. 77
LESSON 2..PG. 84
LESSON 3..PG. 92
CASE STUDY EXERCISES...................PG. 100
FINAL EXAM.......................................PG. 105
AUTHOR BIOGRAPHY.......................PG. 122

Definition: (Webster's) – is both a research area and a practical skill encompassing the ability of an individual or organization to "lead" or guide other individuals, teams, or entire organizations.

LET'S EXAMINE LEADERSHIP!

LEAD

a.) Lead (verb) – cause) (a person or animal) to go with one by-holding them by the hand, a halter (strap), a rope, etc., while moving forward.
b.) Lead (verb) – be in charge or command of.
c.) Lead (noun) – the initiative in an action; an example for others to follow.
d.) Lead (noun) – a position of advantage in a contest; first place.

LEADER

a.) Leader (noun) – something that leads.
b.) Leader (noun) – a person who directs a military force or unit.
c.) Leader (noun) – a person who has commanding authority or influence.
d.) Leader (noun) – a first or principal performer of a group

Which definition(s) best describe you?

_____

_____

_____

_____

How can you apply this in ministry at your church?

_____

_____

_____

_____

Where do you best fit in as a person and what role do you play in the ministry?

_____

_____

_____

SHIP

<u>a.)</u> SHIP (Urban Dictionary) – An unrealistic relationship that you love so much but causes you so much pain and misery forcing you to scream "MY FEELS" while sliding out of your chair because it never comes true though it's so obvious it should.

<u>b.)</u> Martin Luther King, Jr., On Leadership (Donald I. Philips; p. 23) – King said, "Leadership is leaders acting – as well as caring, inspiring and persuading others to act – for certain shared goals that represent the values – the wants and needs, the aspirations and expectations – of themselves and the people they represent.

<u>Leadership lessons from Dr. Martin Luther King, Jr.</u>

Lesson One: You Must Have Total Commitment to Your Cause
Lesson Two: Disrupting the Status Quo Is Essential For Change
Lesson Three: Have A…Then Communicate It And Do It

CLIMBING THE LADDER TO LEADERSHIP

Important Fact: The tallest ladder in the world is 135'-0" tall with 120 rungs! The number 120 can symbolize a divinely appointed time of waiting.

Scriptures:

Genesis 6:1-3 – And it came to pass, when men began to multiply on the face of the earth, and daughters were born unto them,

That the sons of God saw the daughters of men that they were fair; and they took them wives of all which they chose.

And the LORD said, my spirit shall not always strive with man, for that he also is filth; yet his days shall be one hundred and twenty years.

Consider the rungs as _____ _____ of _____; broken down into _____ and _____ levels of leadership each.

The (6) Sections:

1.)_____
2.)_____
3.)_____

4.)_____
5.)_____
6.)_____

The (20) Charcteristics:

1.)_____
2.)_____
3.)_____
4.)_____
5.)_____
6.)_____
7.)_____
8.)_____
9.)_____
10.)_____

11.)_____
12.)_____
13.)_____
14.)_____
15.)_____
16.)_____
17.)_____
18.)_____
19.)_____
20.)_____

Important Facts: Twenty is two times ten and can, at times, be defined as a complete or perfect waiting period!

Scriptures:

Genesis 31:38-41 – This twenty years have I been with thee; thy female sheep and thy she goats have not cast their young, and the rams of thy flock have I not eaten.

That which was torn of beasts I brought not unto thee; I bare the loss of it; of my hand didst thou require it, whether stolen by day, or stolen by night.

Thus I was; in the day the drought consumed me, and the frost by night; and my sleep departed from mine eyes.

Thus have I been twenty years in thy house; I served thee fourteen years for thy two daughters, and six years for thy cattle: and thou hast changed my wages ten times.

Judges 4-5 – For twenty years the children of Israel waited to be freed of Jabin, king of Canaan, who oppressed them. God response was to raise up Deborah and Barak, who freed the people from bondage.

Webster's Definition:
Rung – a horizontal support on a ladder for a person's foot

Leadership's Definition:
Rung – one of the stages or levels in something such as a process or organization through which it is possible to make progress

Each group of the 6 sections has 20 characteristics!

The first section of Climbing the Ladder to Leadership is _____. A good _____ must first construct a _____. This is very vital in the _____ stages of anyone striving to become a good _____. In the _____ of _____ the plan it has to _____ _____. The best _____ understand that others desire their _____ and _____ to be considered and most importantly _____. "Connecting with people is something at which all leaders must excel if they are to be successful." (Martin Luther King, Jr. On leadership Inspiring & Wisdom for Challenging Times; Donald T. Phillips, p. 43)

The one major benefit for any individual who desires to become a leader is _____. So now let's look at the first characteristic which is _____.

Webster's Definition:
Honesty – the quality of being free of deceit and untruthfulness; sincere. One who strives to walk in _____.

Below are some reference scriptures talking about Honesty.

Scriptures:
1 John 3:18 – My little children, let us not love in word, neither in tongue; but in deed and in truth.

Proverbs 11:3 – If the foundations be destroyed, what can the righteous do?

Proverbs 21:3 – To do justice and judgment is more acceptable to the LORD than sacrifice.

Psalms 37:7 – Rest in the LORD, and wait patiently for him: fret not thyself because of him who prospereth in his way, because of the man who bringeth wicked devices to pass.

Psalms 112:5 – A good man sheweth favor, and lendeth: he will guide his affairs with discretion.

Let's look at the second characteristic in Climbing the Ladder to Leadership; which is, _____.

"When leaders listen first, then speak, they are engendering trust in those who would follow."
Martin Luther King, Jr. On leadership Inspiring & Wisdom for Challenging Times; Donald T. Phillips, p. 43

<u>Webster's Definition:</u>

<u>Communication:</u> - the _____ or _____ of information or news.

A good leader must practice being a good _____. One must generate good _____ _____ to become a good leader because the two work together _____ and _____. This _____ with others is _____ in establishing _____. This _____ is needed for one to become a good leader because it _____ to develop a _____ with the _____ of others. This also _____ a structure of _____ and _____ within one's organization! This characteristic plays a vital role in establishing a _____ _____ within the organization. Communicating in _____ _____ helps to establish common _____ with those you are _____.

People tend to _____ together and _____ more when there's a clear _____ of _____ with their leadership!

Now let's see what the Bible has to say about this characteristic.

Scriptures:
John 12:49 – For I have not spoken of myself; but the Father which sent me, he gave me a commandment, what I should say, and what I should speak.

John 17:8 – For I have given unto them the words which thou gavest me; and they have received them, and have known surely that

I came out from thee, and they have believed that thou didst send me.

Acts 4:20 – For we cannot but speak the things which we have seen and heard.

Now take a few minutes to answer the following questions below.

QUESTIONAIRE

How has PREPARATION assisted you in ministry?

_____

_____

_____

_____

What are some things you plan to do for the ministry?

_____

_____

_____

As you are Climbing the Ladder to Leadership, what do these first two characteristics mean to you as a Christian, as a leader, and in your ministry?

_____

_____

_____

_____

Why did God send you to a particular ministry and/or church?

_____

_____

_____

_____

The third characteristic is _____. What does this phrase mean to you? (Open Discussion – 10 minutes)

Webster's Definition:
Delegate – a person sent or authorized to represent others, in particular an elected representative sent to a conference. Entrust (a task or responsibility) to another person, typically one who is less senior than oneself.

A good leader has to have the _____ of others. He or she cannot do it all by themselves. But, a good leader always keeps in mind that he or she is the _____ at all times to go, do, execute whatever it is that need to be done. Also, a good leader when _____, do it with _____ towards others. One must always keep in mind that before he or she became a good leader they were _____ a good _____. A good leader cannot delegate with an _____. This will just cause _____, _____, and _____. When delegating, a good leader must _____ the _____ of a quality of _____ with calm _____ and wise _____ _____.

Emotions must be in _____ and not _____ to appear on the scene. A good leader uses _____ when it comes to delegating and always with _____ towards others. A good leader never stops in being a leader because he understands everything it took to get there. One already has an _____ that it is to the _____.

Dr. Martin Luther King, Jr. once said, "Somebody has to do it and if you think I can, I will serve." A good leader must have a heart of _____. Once that man or that woman make up in his or her mind to _____ _____ of _____ _____ to serve for the _____. When delegating someone for the cause, a good leader will do it with _____ _____.

Martin Luther King, Jr. once said, "When people nominate you for the lead, accept it. When you are asked to serve, you can't say no."

He went on to say, "remember what Hegel wrote: growth comes through pain and struggle."

King also said, "Doing so will inspire sustained involvement of a wide array of individuals."

Fully engage yourself in position for the task that is set before you and do it!

Share some times where you were delegated to complete a task. How was the experience (good or bad)?

Here are a few reference scriptures.

<u>Scriptures:</u>
Titus 1:5 – For this cause left I thee in Crete, that thou shouldest set in order the things that are wanting, and ordain elders in every city, as I had appointed thee:

2 Timothy 2:2 – And the things that thou hast heard of me among many witnesses, the same commit thou to faithful men, who shall be able to teach others also.

James 1:5 – If any of you lack wisdom, let him ask of God, that giveth to all men liberally, and upbraideth not; and it shall be given him.

Romans 13:1-4 – Let every soul be subject unto the higher powers. For there is no power but of God: the powers that be are ordained of God.

Whosoever therefore resisteth the power, resistetth the ordinance of God: and they that resist shall receive to themselves damnation.

For rulers are not a terror to good works, but to the evil. Will thou not be afraid of the power? do that which is good, and thou shalt have praise of the same:

For he is the minister of God to thee for good. But if thou do that which is evil, be afraid; for he beareth not the sword in vain: for he is the minister of God, a revenger to execute wrath upon him that doeth evil.

This will take us to the fourth characteristic; which is, _____. Many _____ and _____ will come when one is walking in this characteristic, especially as a leader!

Webster's Definition:
Confidence – the feeling or belief that one can rely on someone or something; firm trust; the state of feeling certain about the truth of something; a feeling of self-assurance arising from one's appreciation of one's own abilities or qualities.

This characteristic can be a very _____ _____ in a leader's life. This is why is it very important to know why you (the _____) was called to this _____ from the beginning. As you climb the ladder to leadership, you must _____ your Christianity and walk with God because he is the only one who will be able to see you through so _____ the LORD with all your _____.
This is what a good leader will do! Now let's look at some scriptures.

Scriptures:
Micah 7:5 – Trust ye not in a friend, put ye not confidence in a guide: keep the doors of thy mouth from her that lieth in thy bosom.

1 John 5:14 – And this is the confidence that we have in him, that, if we ask any thing according to his will, he heareth us:

2 Chronicles 32:8 – With him is an arm of flesh; but with us is the LORD our God to help us, and to fight our battles. And the people rested themselves upon the words of Hezekiah king of Judah.

Ephesians 3:12 – In whom we have boldness and access with confidence by the faith of him.

The fifth characteristic is, _____.

<u>Webster's Definition:</u>
Commitment – the state or quality of being dedicated to a cause, activity, etc., an engagement or obligation that restricts freedom of action.

_____ is something that need to be exemplified

as a _____ so that when the time comes to be birthed into

_____ ; that individual will have already _____

in that area to a great degree! This characteristic will be

_____ every step of the way, but one has to maintain being _____ for the call. It is definitely a _____ by itself. There will come times where a good leader will want to _____ in the _____, but he or she has to stay _____ on being _____.

Peter M. Senge, author of "The Fifth Discipline" said, "You cannot force commitment, what you can do … You nudge a little here, inspire a little there, and provide a role model. Your primary influence is the environment you create."

He also said, "Courage is simply doing whatever is needed in pursuit of the vision." Another one of his famous quotes is, "The most effective people are those who can hold their vision while remaining committed to seeing current reality clearly."

"The road map for your movement may change, but your final destination should remain the same" (Martin Luther King, Jr. On leadership Inspiring & Wisdom for Challenging Times; Donald T. Phillips, p. 330)

Let's turn our attention to the reference scriptures.

Scriptures:
Joshua 24:14 – Now therefore fear the LORD, and serve him in sincerity and in truth: and put away the gods which your fathers served on the other side of the flood, and in Egypt; and serve ye the LORD.

Acts 2:42 – And they continued stedfastly in the apostles' doctrine and fellowship, and in breaking of bread, and in prayers.

Deuteronomy 13:4 – Ye shall walk after the LORD your God, and fear him, and keep his commandments, and obey his voice, and ye shall serve him, and cleave unto him.

Romans 6:17– But God be thanked, that ye were the servants of sin, but ye   obeyed from the heart that form of doctrine which was delivered you.

Hebrews 11:8 – By faith Abraham, when he was called to go out into a place which he should after receive for an inheritance, obeyed; and he went out, not knowing whither he went.

The sixth characteristic is, _____ _____.

Webster's Definition:

Positive Attitude – having a good effect; favorable; marked by optimism mental position with regard to a fact or state.

A good leader with a positive attitude will_____ a strong _____ within the organization. A good leader has to _____ a positive attitude to be able to _____ every _____ of the _____ in leadership.

"Your aim should be to persuade through love, patience, and understanding good will" "Never seek to defeat or humiliate an opponent. Try to bring about a change of heart." (Martin Luther King, Jr. On leadership Inspiring & Wisdom for Challenging Times; Donald T. Phillips, p. 68)

Press on and keep pressing. If you can't fly, run; if you can't run, walk; if you can't walk – crawl." (Martin Luther King, Jr. On leadership Inspiring & Wisdom for Challenging Times; Donald T. Phillips, p. 121)

"A Positive Attitude leads to success and happiness and helps you cope easily with the everyday cares of life. It also brings optimism into a good leader's life, and makes it easier to avoid worries and negative thinking." (www.successconsciousness.com)

Let's see what the scriptures have to say!

<u>Scriptures:</u>
Philippians 4:8 – Finally, brethren, whatsoever things are true, whatsoever things are honest, whatsoever things are just, whatsoever things are pure, whatsoever things are lovely, whatsoever things are of good report; if there be any virtue, and if there be any praise, think on these things.

Jeremiah 29:11 – For I know the things that I think toward you, saith the LORD, thoughts of peace, and not of evil, to give you an expected end.

Proverbs 18:21 – Death and life are in the power of the tongue: and they that love it shall eat the fruit thereof.

Romans 12:2 – And be not conformed to this world: but be ye transformed by the renewing of your mind, that ye may prove what is that good, and acceptable, and perfect, will of God.

Proverbs 12:22 – A merry heart doeth good like a medicine: but a broken spirit drieth the bones.

The seventh characteristic to Climbing the Ladder to Leadership is_____.

Webster's Definition: ___

Intuition – the ability to _____ something _____, without the need for conscious reasoning; a thing that one knows or considers likely from _____ feeling rather than _____ reasoning.

A good leader must spend adequate time _____ and _____.

Peter M. Senge, author of "The Fifth Discipline" said, "People with high levels of personal mastery … cannot afford to choose between reason and intuition, or head and heart, any more than they would choose to walk on one leg or see with one eye." (www.quotter.net)

Peter M. Senge also said, "New insights fail to get put into practice because they conflict with deeply held internal images of how the world works … images that limit us to familiar ways of thinking and acting. That is why the discipline of managing mental models – surfacing, testing, and improving our internal picture of how the world works – promises to be a major breakthrough for learning organization." (www.quotter.net)

Martin Luther King, Jr. said, "Remember that many issues you have not cleared up intellectually may be solved in the sphere of practical action and experience." He went on to say, "Create a blueprint for yourself – one that you can utilize in your future leadership endeavors. Become your own teacher." (Martin Luther King, Jr. On leadership Inspiring & Wisdom for Challenging Times; Donald T. Phillips, p. 68)

Let's turn our attention to a few scripture references.

Scriptures:
Proverbs 2:6-8 – For the LORD giveth wisdom: out of his mouth cometh knowledge and understanding.
He layeth up sound wisdom for the righteous: he is a buckler to them that walk uprightly.

He keepeth the paths of judgment, and preserveth the way of his saints.

2 Timothy 3:16 – All scripture is given by inspiration of God, and is profitable for doctrine, for reproof, for correction, for instruction in

righteousness.

John 16:33 – These things I have spoken unto you, that in me ye might have peace. In the world ye shall have tribulation: but be of good cheer; I have overcome the world.

The eighth characteristic is _____.

<u>Webster's Definition:</u>
Creativity – the use of the imagination or original ideas, especially in the production of an artistic work.

Generate a thorough _____ of every major _____. Share it with those who are a part of your _____. Generate a list of things to be done _____ and use it as a _____ for future action. _____ generating _____, _____ and _____ to help drive your leadership to the next_____. New _____ should always be _____ within any leadership. Even entertain the _____ of others in your organization.

Martin Luther King, Jr. said, "Subject yourself to endless self-analysis so as to be certain that you are fulfilling the true meaning of your work, maintaining your sense of purpose, holding fast to your ideas, and guiding people in the right direction. Make good use of your downtime. Go somewhere so that you may think about things." (Martin Luther King, Jr. On leadership Inspiring & Wisdom for Challenging Times; Donald T. Phillips, p. 86)

This is what the Bible says about this characteristic.

Scriptures:
Exodus 35:31-33 – And he hath filled him with the spirit of God, in wisdom, in understanding, and in knowledge, and in all manner of workmanship;

And to devise curious works, to work in gold, and in silver, and in brass,

And in the cutting of stones, to set them, and in carving of wood, to make any manner of cunning work.

Ephesians 2:10 – For we are his workmanship, created in Christ Jesus unto good works, which God hath before ordained that we should walk in them.

1 Kings 3:12 – Behold, I have done according to thy words: lo, I have given thee a wise and an understanding heart; so that there was none like thee before thee, neither after thee shall any arise like unto thee.

Proverbs 22:29 – Seest thou a man diligent in his business? he shall stand before kings; he shall not stand before mean men.

Colossians 3:23-24 – And whatsoever ye do, do it heartily, as to the LORD, and not unto men;

Knowing that of the LORD ye shall receive the reward of the inheritance: for ye serve the LORD Christ.

The ninth characteristic is, _____.

Webster's Definition:

Sense of Humor – the ability to_____ _____ or appreciate a joke.

A good leader definitely needs to _____ this characteristic because he or she will _____ _____ and _____ _____ from all types of people. One must be able to _____ at the _____ and _____ and _____ on. A good leader also needs to be _____ in this characteristic for the sake of _____.

Martin Luther King, Jr. said, "When you fail to keep people motivated and inspired, they may complain or "throw rocks" in desperation" (Martin Luther King, Jr. On leadership Inspiring & Wisdom For Challenging Times; Donald T. Phillips, p. 86)

Scriptures:
Luke 6:21 – Blessed are ye that hunger now: for ye shall be filled. Blessed are ye that weep now: for ye shall laugh.

Job 8:21 – Till he fill thy mouth with laughing, and thy lips with rejoicing.

Psalms 126:2-3 – Then was our mouth filled with laughter, and our tongue with singing: then said they among the heathen, the LORD hath done great things for them.

The LORD hath done great things for us; whereof we are glad.

As we approach the half way point of Climbing the Ladder to Leadership, let us look the tenth characteristic; which is _____.

Webster's Definition:

Ability to Inspire – to make someone have a particular feeling or react in a particular way; make people feel confident because they trust your ability.

As a leader, constantly speak about the _____ and _____ of those apart of your organization with _____, _____, and _____. A good leader must _____ _____ for _____.

Martin Luther King, Jr. said, "Your aim should be to persuade through love, patience, and understanding good will." (Martin Luther King, Jr. On leadership Inspiring & Wisdom for Challenging Times; Donald T. Phillips, p. 68)

As people began to derive inspiration from their involvement, I realized that the choice leaves your own hands. The people expect you to give them leadership" (Martin Luther King, Jr. On leadership Inspiring & Wisdom for Challenging Times; Donald T. Phillips, p. 50

Below are a few scripture references.

<u>Scriptures:</u>
1 Samuel 10:7 – And let it be, when these signs are come unto thee, that thou do as occasion serve thee; for God is with thee.

Ecclesiastes 9:10 – Whatsoever thy hand findeth to do, do it with thy might; for there is no work, nor device, nor knowledge, nor wisdom, in the grave, whither thou goest.

Galatians 6:9 – And let us not be weary in well doing: for in due season we shall reap, if we faint not.

Proverbs 16:3 – Commit thy works unto the LORD, and thy thoughts shall be established.

We have reached the halfway point of Climbing the Ladder to Leadership in conjunction with the first section; which is, PREPARATION! Let's now look at the diagram below.

Diagram 1

POSITIONED @ THE HALFWAY POINT OF CLIMBING THE LADDER TO LEADERSHIP

As we have reached the halfway point, let's focus on the eleventh characteristic _____.

"Do it because it is right to do it." (Martin Luther King, Jr. On leadership Inspiring & Wisdom for Challenging Times; Donald T. Phillips, p. 122

<u>Webster's Definition:</u>

Responsibility – the _____ or _____ of having _____ to deal with something or of having _____ over someone; the state or fact of being _____ to blame for something; the _____ or _____ to act _____ and make _____ without _____.

Notice now how the _____ _____ of our Climbing the Ladder to Leadership started out with _____ and the second half is starting out with _____. Isn't this _____; a good leader must at all times take _____ for his or her_____. This is very _____ and _____ for any leadership to be able to _____ _____. A good leader will _____ _____ _____ without _____ for others. There is always an _____ that he or she _____ be _____.

Taking _____ requires any good leader to _____ the _____ apart of the organization _____ and _____ of _____ that has _____ within the organization.

"There comes a time when one must take the position that it is neither safe nor politic nor popular, but he must do it because his conscience tells him it is right." (Martin Luther King, Jr. On leadership Inspiring & Wisdom For Challenging Times; Donald T. Phillips, p. 176)

A good leader has the _____ to always _____ _____ and always _____ _____ within the organization. He or she also _____ on responsibility _____ the ability to _____ _____ of any _____. When a good leader makes up in his or her mind of taking responsibility, he

or she is _____ to do _____ that _____ the cause.
Good _____ demands a good leader to always be _____ and do the right thing. Always _____ _____ and _____ _____.

"We must demonstrate, teach, and preach, until the very foundation of our nation are shaken." (Martin Luther King, Jr. On leadership Inspiring & Wisdom for Challenging Times; Donald T. Phillips, p. 197)

Let's now reference the Bible for some scriptures dealing with responsibility.

<u>Scriptures:</u>
Genesis 6:5-6 – And God saw that the wickedness of man was great in the earth, and that every imagination of the thoughts of his heart was only evil continually. And it repented the LORD that he had made man on the earth, and it grieved him at his heart.

Matthew 12:37 – For by thy words thou shalt be justified, and by thy words thou shalt be condemned.

Luke 16:10 – He that is faithful in that which is least is faithful also in much: and he that is unjust in the least is unjust also in much.

Genesis 3:12-13 – And the man said, The woman whom thou gavest to be with me, she gave me of the tree, and I did eat.
And the LORD God said unto the woman, What is this that thou hast done? And the woman said, The serpent beguiled me, and I did eat.

1 Samuel 15:22 – And Samuel said, Hath the LORD as great delight in burnt offerings and sacrifices, as in obeying the voice of the LORD? Behold, to obey is better than sacrifice, and to hearken than the fat of rams.

The twelfth characteristic is _____.

What does this characteristic mean to you and why is this one so critical for one who is Climbing the Ladder to Leadership? (Open Discussion – 10 Minutes)

Webster's Definition:

Spirituality – something that in _____ law belongs to the church or to a priest or religious leader; sensitivity or attachment to religious values; clergy.

A good leader, on a _____ _____ will always _____ to do the following:

1.) _____ _____ on the Word of God!

2.) _____ _____ that God will _____ _____ _____!

3.) _____ to be a good _____ in _____ and of a good _____ that he or she may _____ to be _____ by God!

4.) _____ the _____ to be there for the _____!

5.) _____ to _____ keep the _____ _____!

A good leader should _____ to _____ these (5) things in his or her _____. For any good leader to _____ in the _____ _____, he or she should have a _____ _____ _____ with the LORD! He or she will _____ their _____ _____ into all _____ of their life. This will _____ more _____ in living and _____to a_____ _____ lifestyle. Those who don't _____ their _____ with the _____ of their life _____ _____.

A good spiritual leader is _____ with _____ _____ _____ his or her day and within their organization. _____ _____ teaches a good leader that it is the _____ that _____ and not how _____ _____ to what you do. A good spiritual leader always has a _____ _____ on the _____ of his or her life. He or she always _____ _____ _____, but never lose _____ _____. Hope _____ and _____ a good leader and it causes others to _____ within the organization.

"The forces that threaten to negate life must be challenged by courage … This requires the exercise of a creative will that enables us to hew out a stone of hope from a mountain of despair." (Martin Luther King, Jr. On leadership Inspiring & Wisdom for Challenging Times; Donald T. Phillips, p. 310)

Now let's look at some scriptures that talk about this characteristic of SPIRITUALITY.

Scriptures:
Romans 8:4 & 6 – That the righteousness of the law might be fulfilled in us, who walk not after the flesh, but after the Spirit.

For to be carnally minded is death; but to be spiritually minded is life and peace.

John 6:27 - Labour not for the meat which perisheth, but for the meat which endureth unto everlasting life, which the Son of man shall dive unto you: for him hath God the Father sealed.

Joshua 22:5 – But take diligent heed to do the commandment and the law, which Moses the servant of the LORD charged you, to love the LORD your God, and to walk in all his ways, and to keep his commandments, and to cleave unto him, and to serve him with all your heart and with all your soul.

Psalms 1:2 – But his delight is in the law of the LORD; and in his law doth he meditate day and night.

1 Kings 8:23 – And he said, LORD God of Israel, there is no God like thee, in heaven above, or on earth beneath, who keepest covenant and mercy with thy servants that walk before thee with all their heart.

Now we will be looking at the thirteenth characteristic; which is
_____.

A good leader will _____ the _____ _____ of others within the organization, but he or she know not to _____ _____ to get the _____ of them. A good leader should be able to _____ without being _____ with others within the organization.

"We can differ and still unite around common goals." (Martin Luther King, Jr. On leadership Inspiring & Wisdom for Challenging Times; Donald T. Phillips, p. 154)

Webster's Definition:

Sensitivity – the quality or condition of being sensitive; a lack of common decency and sensitivity; a person's feelings which might be easily offended or hurt; sensibilities.

"We must not become bitter; nor must we harbor the desire to retaliate with violence." (Martin Luther King, Jr. On leadership Inspiring & Wisdom for Challenging Times; Donald T. Phillips, p. 177)

A good leader must be _____ as well as _____. He or she must _____ being a _____ as well as an _____. A good leader must always keep his or her _____ _____. One cannot allow _____ to cause _____ to _____ their leadership.

"Leaders act for the wants and needs, the aspirations, and expectations of the people they represent." (Martin Luther King, Jr. On leadership Inspiring & Wisdom for Challenging Times; Donald T. Phillips, p. 229)

This is the _____ that a good leader will _____ within his or her organization. A good leader will also put his or her own self in _____ that will _____ him or her to _____ the _____ and _____ the _____ of the people who are being represented. A good leader will _____ _____ time with the people in their organization. This will _____ an _____ of their _____ _____.

Next are a few reference scriptures.

Scriptures:

Judges 2:18 – And when the LORD raised them up judges, then the LORD was with the judge, and delivered them out of the hand of their enemies all the days of the judge: for it repented the LORD because of their groanings by reason of them that oppressed them and vexed them.

Lamentations 3:22 – It is the LORD's mercies that we are not consumed, because his compassions fail not."

Luke 13:34 – O Jerusalem, Jerusalem, which killest the prophets, and stonest them that are sent unto thee; how often would I have gathered thy children together, as a hen doth gather her brood (family of young animals) under her wings, and ye would not!

Luke 19:41 – And when he was come near, he beheld the city, and wept over it,

Hebrews 2:18 – For in that he himself hath suffered being tempted, he is able to succour (assistance and support in times of hardship and distress) them that are tempted.

Romans 12:15 – Rejoice with them that do rejoice, and weep with them that weep.

How do you see yourself handling this characteristic as a leader?

_____

_____

_____

_____

_____

The fourteenth characteristic is _____.

Collaboration – the action of working with someone to produce or create something; traitorous cooperation with an enemy.

Why is this characteristic important when it comes to leadership?

_____

_____

_____

_____

A good leader must always _____ that _____ who is apart of the organization is _____ on his or her leadership. Good _____ _____. A good leader _____ with the _____ within their organization, but _____ makes any _____ _____ without the ____ of _____ in the organization. This kind of _____ from _____ will _____ _____ _____ of a _____ of _____.

J. Paul Getty once said, "I would rather have one percent of the effort of one hundred people than one hundred percent of my own."

A good leader will always take the time to _____ why his or her _____, he or she is always _____ to _____ and _____ _____ _____. Leadership is always _____ that ____ must be used _____ because time is of the _____.

"Action is not in itself a virtue; its goals and its forms determine its value." (Martin Luther King, Jr. On leadership Inspiring & Wisdom for Challenging Times; Donald T. Phillips, p. 175)

"When there is friction between two important groups in your organization, create a joint initiative involving both and hold daily meetings to beef up communication and increase teamwork." (Martin Luther King, Jr. On leadership Inspiring & Wisdom for Challenging Times; Donald T. Phillips, p. 216)

A good leader must _____ _____ _____ to _____.

One also understands that _____ is _____

When _____ is _____ an _____ and _____ situation, a good leader will make a _____ attempt to _____ the conditions because he or she always _____ they have a _____!

"Tell the people that you either go up together, or you go down together." (Martin Luther King, Jr. On leadership Inspiring & Wisdom for Challenging Times; Donald T. Phillips, p. 330)

Consider these scripture references.

<u>Scriptures:</u>
Proverbs 14:15 – The simple believeth every word: but the prudent (wise) man looketh well to his going.

Isaiah 52:7 – How beautiful upon the mountains are the feet of him that bringeth good tidings, that publisheth peace; that bringeth good tidings of good, that publisheth salvation; that saith unto Zion, Thy God reigneth!

Psalms 45:7 – Thou lovest righteousness, and hatest wickedness: therefore God, thy God, hath anointed thee with the oil of gladness above thy fellows.

Nehemiah 5:16-17 – Yea, also I continued in thy work of this wall, neither bought we any land: and all my servants were gathered thither unto the work.

Moreover there were at my table an hundred and fifty of the Jews and rulers, beside those that came unto us from among the heathen that are about us.

Genesis 1:27 – So God created man in his own image, in the image of God created he him; male and female created he them.

2 Peter 1:21 – For the prophecy came not in old time by the will of man: but holy men of God spake as they were moved by the Holy Ghost.

The fifteenth characteristic is _____.

Webster's Definition:
Genuine – truly what something is said to be: authentic; (of a person, emotion, or action) sincere.

A good leader strives to always _____ from his or her _____.

"Subject yourself to endless self-analysis so as to be certain that you are fulfilling the true meaning of your work, maintaining your sense of purpose, holding fast to your ideals, and guiding people in the right direction." (Martin Luther King, Jr. On leadership Inspiring & Wisdom for Challenging Times; Donald T. Phillips, p. 86)

A good leader is always _____ to _____ the question "What would you do!" He or she will be _____ in _____ it _____; that is, being _____. It is _____ for _____ to _____ this _____ to the _____.

"Within the best of people there is some evil, and within the worst there is some good." (Martin Luther King, Jr. On leadership Inspiring & Wisdom for Challenging Times; Donald T. Phillips, p. 274)

"Ultimately, a genuine leader is not a searcher for consensus, but a molder of consensus. I would rather be a man of conviction than a man of conformity." (Martin Luther King, Jr. On leadership Inspiring & Wisdom for Challenging Times; Donald T. Phillips, p. 176)

A good leader who is genuine always _____ his or her _____ by their _____ and it will be heard.

"The people are looking to me for leadership, ___ and if I stand before them without strength and courage, they will falter." (Martin Luther King, Jr. On leadership Inspiring & Wisdom for Challenging Times; Donald T. Phillips, p. 330).

A genuine leader will have _____ _____ _____ the people and his or her organization. It is _____ for _____ to be _____. In general, a leader _____ to be _____ _____ a strong _____ to _____ _____. One even strives to be genuine in his or her _____ _____ in their leadership.

53

A genuine good leader will _____ to allow the _____ to _____ in his or her _____ _____ so that the leadership will be _____ _____.

Let us now look at some scriptures for reference.

<u>Scriptures:</u>
1 Samuel 16:7 – But the LORD said unto Samuel, Look not on his countenance, or on the height of his stature; because I have refused him: for the LORD seeth not as man seeth; for man looketh on the outward appearance, but the LORD looketh on the heart.

Proverbs 16:3 – Commit thy works unto the LORD, and thy thoughts shall be established.

Jeremiah 29:11 – For I know the thoughts that I think toward you, saith the LORD, thoughts of peace, and not of evil, to give you an expected end.

1 Peter 5:6 – Humble yourselves therefore under the mighty hand of God, that he may exalt you in due time:

1 Corinthians 15:10 – But by the grace of God I am what I am: and his grace which was bestowed upon me was not in vain; but I

labored more abundantly than they all: yet not I, but the grace of God which was with me.

The sixteenth characteristic is _____.

<u>Webster's Definition:</u>
Supportive – providing encouragement or emotional help.

"When you fail to keep people motivated and inspired, they may complain or throw rocks in desperation." (Martin Luther King, Jr. On leadership Inspiring & Wisdom for Challenging Times; Donald T. Phillips, p. 86)

A good leader will spend_____ _____ _____ _____ of character into the _____ of those apart of the organization. He or she is always _____ with other members of their organization. Taking the time to _____ the people in his or her organization; _____ their _____ a more _____ team. This _____ to the _____ of _____. Inspiring those a part of the leadership to continue to _____ _____. Good leadership understands that _____ _____ to _____ has to always come from _____ _____ _____ and mind of each individual who is a part of the _____ and _____.

"Good leadership realize this fact and attempt to tap into the internal desires of the people they represent." (Martin Luther King, Jr. On leadership Inspiring & Wisdom for Challenging Times; Donald T. Phillips, p. 111)

A good leader always strives to _____ _____ of _____ and _____ a _____ within his or her organization. Sometimes there are even _____ available within the organization to be of an _____. _____ leadership sets the _____ for people in the organization. Having a _____ _____ structure within any organization _____, _____ and _____.

"Teams bring together a broader mix of skills that exceed those of any single individual." (Martin Luther King, Jr. On leadership Inspiring & Wisdom for Challenging Times; Donald T. Phillips, p. 147)

This is why it is _____ for any good leader to be _____ towards those who are part of the organization. They will _____ _____ to be _____ to their leaders.

Martin Luther King, Jr. once said, "When one person stands up, he may be run out of town but when a thousand stand up together the situation is drastically altered." (Martin Luther King, Jr. On leadership Inspiring & Wisdom for Challenging Times; Donald T. Phillips, p. 153)

A good leader will, even _____ a _____ _____ _____ _____ for individuals within the organization. This is being supportive as a good leader.

"There comes a time when people get tired of being flung across the abyss of humiliation where they experience the bleakness of nagging despair." (Martin Luther King, Jr. On leadership Inspiring & Wisdom for Challenging Times; Donald T. Phillips, p. 267

"People fail to get along with each other because they fear each other ___ and they fear each other because they don't know each other." (Martin Luther King, Jr. On leadership Inspiring & Wisdom for Challenging Times; Donald T. Phillips, p. 274)

Consider the Bible scriptures below.

Scriptures:
1 Thessalonians 5:11 – Wherefore comfort yourselves together, and edify one another, even as also ye do.

Ephesians 4:29 – Let no corrupt communication proceed out of your mouth, but that which is good to the use of edifying, that it may minister grace unto the hearers.

Hebrews 10:24 – And let us consider one another to provoke unto love and to good works:

Proverbs 27:17 – Iron sharpeneth iron; so a man sharpeneth the countenance of his friend.

Proverbs 12:25 – Heaviness in the heart of man maketh it stoop: but a good word maketh it glad.

Isaiah 1:17 – Learn to do well; seek judgment, relieve the oppressed, judge the fatherless, plead for the widow.

What are some ways your leadership has been supportive to you and some ways you have been supportive to your leadership? (Open Discussion – 10 Minutes)

The seventeenth characteristic is _____.

<u>Webster's Definition:</u>

Relationship – the way in which two or more concepts, objects, or people are connected, or the state of being connected; the state of being connected by blood or marriage; the way in which two or more people or organizations regard and behave toward each other.

Peter M. Senge once said, "When people in organizations focus only on their position, they have little sense of responsibility for the results produced when all positions interact. Moreover, when results are disappointing, it can be very difficult to know why. All you can do is assume that "someone screwed up." (The Fifth Discipline: The Art & Practice of the Learning Organization)

This is why good leaders will _____ everyone through _____, _____, and _____. No organization can make it _____. A good leader will spend a _____ _____ _____ putting together a _____ team; _____ _____ _____ with everyone on the team. This is a _____ of _____ leadership.

"This teamwork process involves many working members of an organization." (Martin Luther King, Jr. On leadership Inspiring & Wisdom for Challenging Times; Donald T. Phillips, p. 147)

A good leader _____ his or her organization with people of _____ _____. By doing such, he or she _____ a _____ within the organization by _____ a _____ of _____ and _____. This model of _____ is an _____ _____ _____ for any good leader to share with those who are a part of the organization.

"We are tied together in the single garment of destiny, caught in an inescapable network of mutuality. And whatever affects one directly affects all indirectly." (Martin Luther King, Jr. On leadership Inspiring & Wisdom for Challenging Times; Donald T. Phillips, p. 152)

A good leader _____ his or her organization by _____ _____ with his or her _____.

"Knowing how his people will react in any given situation, how they may be inspired and motivated, and how they will behave no matter what a leader does, is a critical skill for effective leadership." (Martin Luther King, Jr. On leadership Inspiring & Wisdom for Challenging Times; Donald T. Phillips, p. 269)

This is why, through _____ a good leader will _____ his or her people within the organization. One will also _____ _____ with his or her people within the organization.

"If you can't stop for an average person in your organization, then you don't need to pursue your lofty goals." (Martin Luther King, Jr. On leadership Inspiring & Wisdom for Challenging Times; Donald T. Phillips, p.330)

Scriptures:

Proverbs 13:20 – He that walketh with wise men shall be wise: but a companion of fools shall be destroyed.

Colossians 3:23 – And whatsoever ye do, do it heartily, as to the Lord, and not unto men;

2 Corinthians 6:14 – Be ye not unequally yoked together with unbelievers: for what fellowship hath righteousness with unrighteousness? And what communion hath light with darkness?

Proverbs 18:24 – A man that hath friends must shew himself friendly: and there is a friend that sticketh closer than a brother.

Isaiah 43:10 - Ye are my witnesses, saith the LORD, and my servants whom I have chosen: that ye may know and believe me, and understand that I am he: before me there was no God formed, neither shall there be after me.

The eighteenth characteristic is _____.

Webster's definition:

Seriousness – the quality of being serious.

A good leader _____ in this characteristic will _____ _____ _____; while _____ support for his or her _____. One _____ his or her leadership; like running a _____. This is the _____ that is being _____. The _____ that a good leader _____ his or her organization will _____ how it is _____ by others.

"I question and self-search constantly into myself to be as certain as I can that I am fulfilling the true meaning of my work, that I am maintaining my sense of purpose, that I am holding fast to my ideas, that I am guiding my people in the right direction." (Martin Luther King, Jr. On leadership Inspiring & Wisdom for Challenging Times; Donald T. Phillips, p.77)

A good leader is _____ _____ his or her _____ to strengthen their leadership. One will experience a lot of _____ _____ _____ _____. He or she always has the _____ of their leadership as _____ _____.

"If America is to remain a first-class nation, it cannot have a second-class citizenship." (Martin Luther King, Jr. On leadership

Inspiring & Wisdom for Challenging Times; Donald T. Phillips, p.103)

"This is a time of action" (Martin Luther King, Jr. On leadership Inspiring & Wisdom for Challenging Times; Donald T. Phillips, p.111)

A good leader _____ _____ of _____ _____, _____, and _____ _____ to his or her organization, so that everyone will know the _____ of _____.

"A good leader gets around quickly and people will follow their leader when something new is proven effective." (Martin Luther King, Jr. On leadership Inspiring & Wisdom for Challenging Times; Donald T. Phillips, p.132)

A good leader will _____, _____, _____ and face the _____ of _____. _____ leadership _____ one to take on a_____ _____ as a leader of any organization.

64

"Leaders blaze no trails. They plow new ground. They sail uncharted waters. Leaders are out in front." (Martin Luther King, Jr. On leadership Inspiring & Wisdom for Challenging Times; Donald T. Phillips, p.263)

A good leader always walks in an _____ of _____ towards those in his or her organization. This generates that _____ to act upon the people; _____ with them, _____ _____ in their _____ and _____ their _____, _____, _____, _____, and _____. A good leader is _____ about having a _____ leadership.

"True compassion is more than flinging a coin to a beggar." (Martin Luther King, Jr. On leadership Inspiring & Wisdom for Challenging Times; Donald T. Phillips, p.290)

One takes on this characteristic of _____ where he or she will _____ to _____ the people within the organization. They are like _____.

Reference the next few scriptures.

Scriptures:

Titus 2:7 – In all things shewing thyself a pattern of good works: in doctrine shewing uncorruptness, gravity (seriousness), sincerity,

1 Timothy 3:14-15 – These things write I unto thee, hoping to come unto thee shortly; But if I tarry long, that thou mayest know how thou oughtest to behave thyself in the house of God, which is the church of the living God, the pillar and ground of the truth.

Proverbs 16:20 – He that handleth a matter wisely shall find good: and whoso trusteth in the LORD, happy is he.

Matthew 6:33 – But seek ye first the kingdom of God, and his righteousness; and all these things shall be added unto you.

The nineteenth characteristic is _____.

Webster's Definition:

Admiration – respect and warm approval; something regarded as impressive or worthy of respect; pleasurable contemplation.

This is done with all _____, _____, and _____.

Good leadership must have _____ within the organization.

A good leader is always _____ about the _____ of the people within the organization. He or she always starts the day _____ every morning to _____ _____ _____ than the _____.

"They are continually giving a little encouragement when things are going well ___ and a lot of encouragement when things are not going well." (Martin Luther King, Jr. On leadership Inspiring & Wisdom for Challenging Times; Donald T. Phillips, p.118)

The _____ _____ of this _____ is to keep _____ _____ in the _____ and to _____ with the motto, "_____ _____"

To those who are a part of the organization. This characteristic _____ to _____ and _____ others within the _____. A _____ of _____ will begin to _____ throughout the _____ organization.

Leadership is _____ _____ when _____ is constantly being _____ within the organization.

Where there is _____, you will find _____! This is _____ for any leadership to be _____.

"Power is the ability to achieve purpose." (Martin Luther King, Jr. On leadership Inspiring & Wisdom for Challenging Times; Donald T. Phillips, p.193)

"Deep down within all of us, [we have] an instinct, it's a kind of drum major instinct – a desire to be out front, a desire to lead the people, a desire to be first." (Martin Luther King, Jr. On leadership Inspiring & Wisdom for Challenging Times; Donald T. Phillips, p.273)

_____ within a leadership will _____ to others within the organization to _____. A good leadership must have an _____ of an _____, and _____ _____ within the organization. Such a _____ _____ will _____ _____ _____ of _____, _____, and _____ of _____ within _____ who are a part of the organization.

68

"If a leader is going to be successful, however, a compassionate and caring nature must be combined with a strong desire to achieve." (Martin Luther King, Jr. On leadership Inspiring & Wisdom for Challenging Times; Donald T. Phillips, p.288)

A good leader always _____ to _____ _____ _____ his or her people within the organization.

Let us now look at some scriptures about the characteristic.

Scriptures:
Proverbs 20:29 – The glory of young men is their strength: and the beauty of old men is the grey head.

Hebrews 12:2 – Looking unto Jesus the author and finisher of our faith; who for the joy that was set before him endured the cross, despising the shame, and is set down at the right hand of the throne of God.

The final characteristic is _____.

Webster's Definition:

Concrete- a heavy, rough building material made from a mixture of broken stone or gravel, sand, cement, and water, that can be spread or poured into molds and that forms a stone like mass on hardening; cover (an area) with concrete; form (something) into a mass; solidify.

We have learned from the beginning, that a good leader who is Climbing the Ladder to Leadership _____ first; start with a _____, but _____ his or her leadership _____ must _____ _____. _____ concrete is _____ to the _____ of any organization being able to _____ and _____ through _____ type of _____.

There will be rocky places of frustration and meandering points of bewilderment. There will be inevitable setbacks here and there." (Martin Luther King, Jr. On leadership Inspiring & Wisdom for Challenging Times; Donald T. Phillips, p.311)

Good Leadership need to be _____ about its _____, _____, _____, and etc. In other words, the _____ needs to have a _____ _____.

Why is this characteristic important for a leader to possess?

_____

_____

_____

_____

_____

Good leadership strives to be _____, and _____ to _____ _____ that may happen; it's _____.

Sometimes _____ can only _____ their _____ with _____ _____.

"A productive and happy life is not something that you find; it is something that you make. (Martin Luther King, Jr. On leadership Inspiring & Wisdom for Challenging Times; Donald T. Phillips, p.216)

A good leader has to be _____ about the _____ and _____ and the _____ of his or her leadership and organization. One of the greatest _____ for any leadership and organization is _____ _____ and _____ it _____. A _____ leadership creates _____ within the leadership.

Take a moment to consider the following scriptures.

Scriptures:
Genesis 44:12 – And he searched, and began at the eldest, and left at the youngest: and the cup was found in Benjamin's sack.

Ezra 6:1 – Then Darius the king made a decree, and search was made in the house of the rolls, where the treasures were laid up in Babylon.

Leviticus 10:16 – And Moses diligently sought the goat of the sin offering, and, behold, it was burnt: and he was angry with Eleazar and Ithamar, the sons of Aaron which were left alive, saying,

Luke 13:7 – Then said he unto the dresser of his vineyard, Behold, these three years I come seeking fruit on the fig tree, and find none: cut it down; why cumbereth it the ground?

Mark 10:45 – For even the Son of man came not to be ministered unto, but to minister, and to give his life a ransom for many.

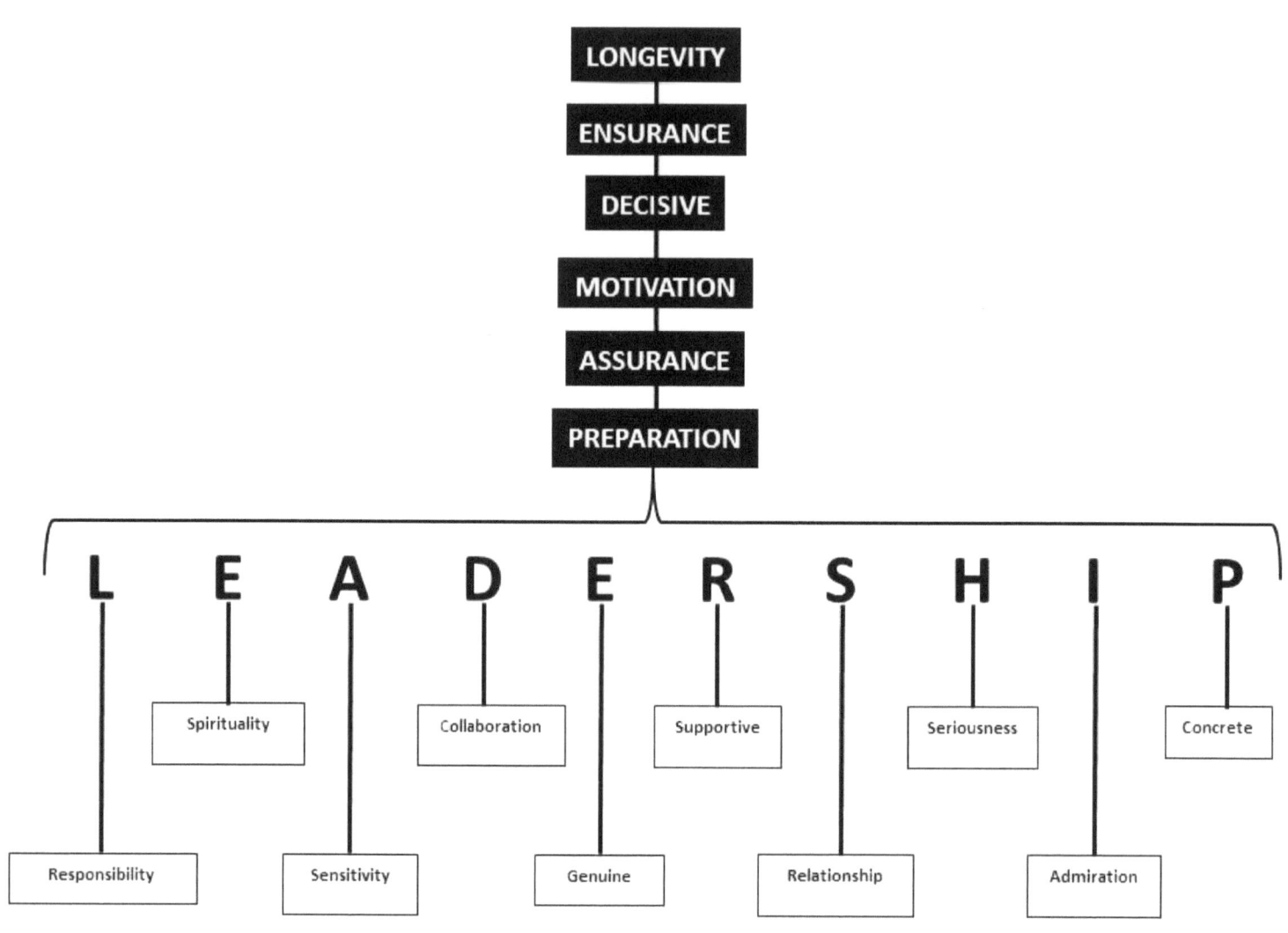

Diagram 2

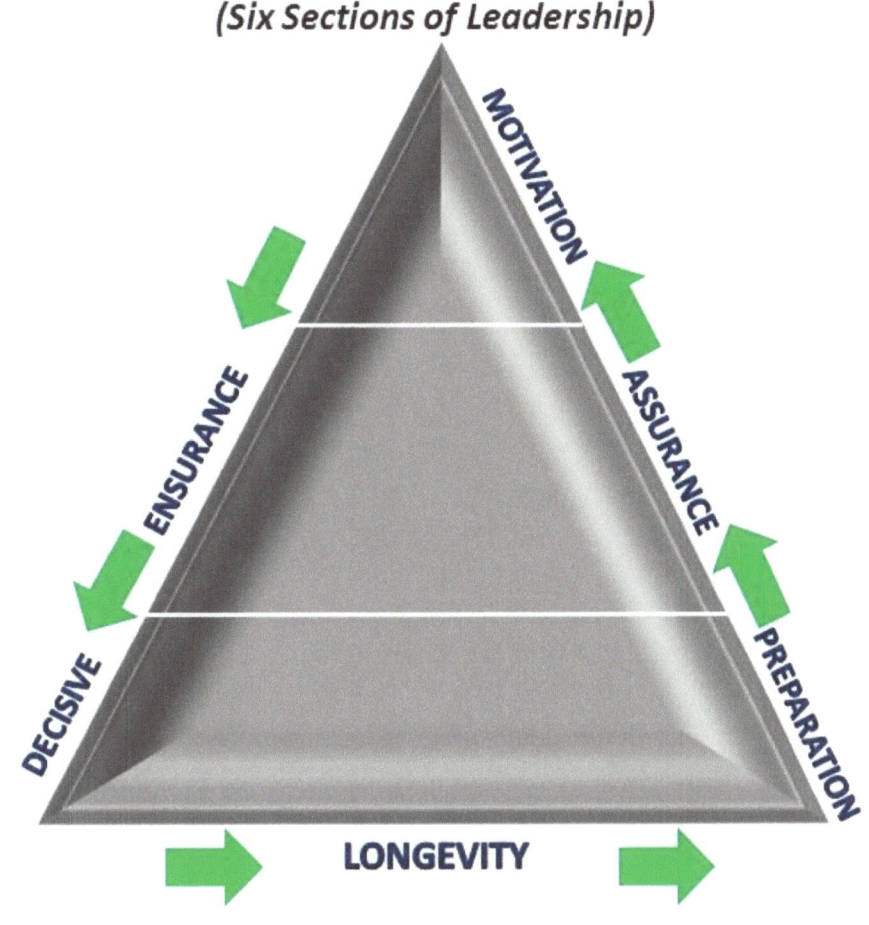

Diagram 3

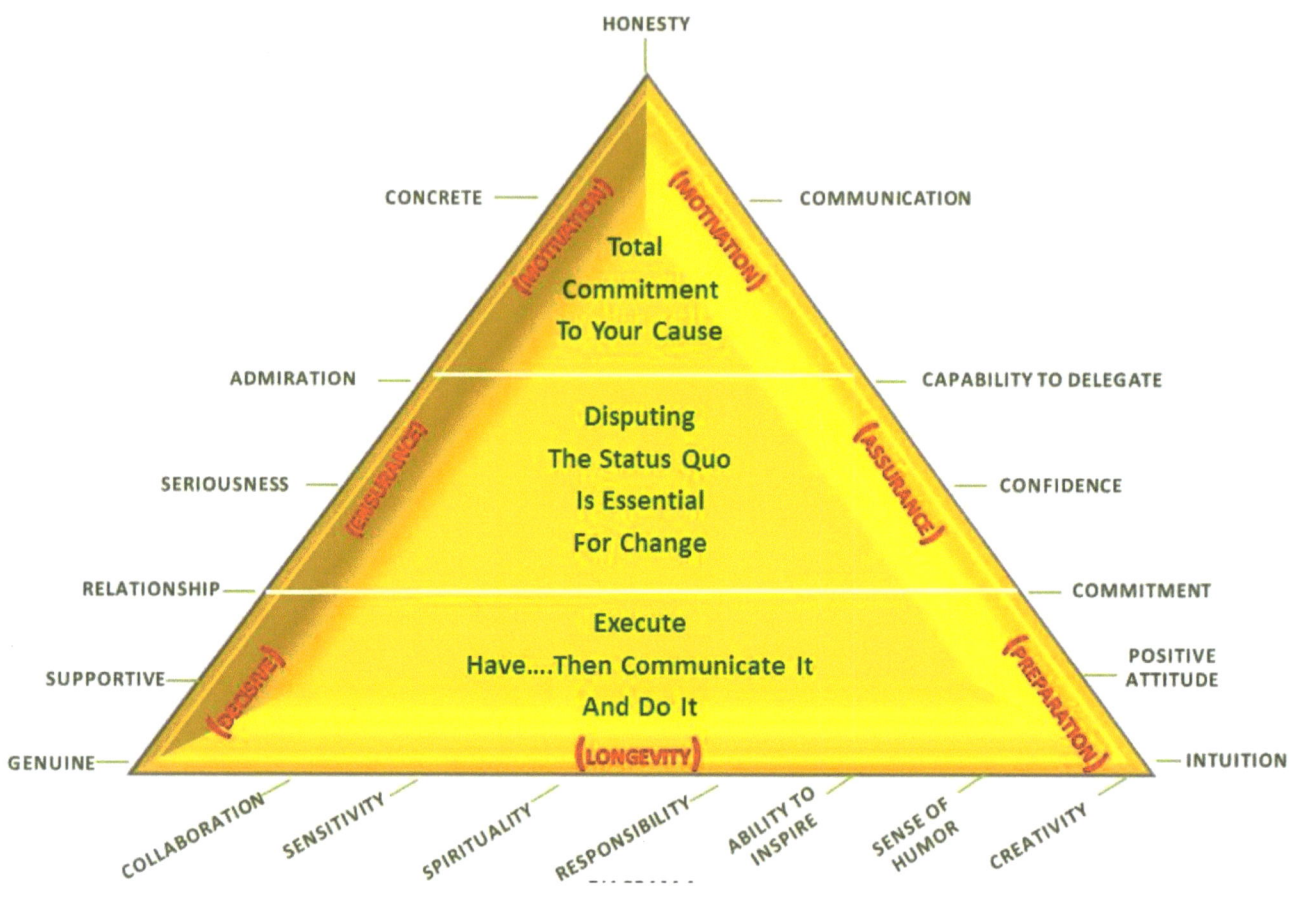

Diagram 4

_____ must have _____ _____ to _____ _____.
In looking at the PYRAMID TO CLIMB THE LADDER TO LEADERSHIP; (Diagram 4 page 76): there are _____ _____ that must be _____ with the _____ _____. This _____ has to be _____ and _____ on a _____ _____ for any leadership to _____ _____ _____ to his or her _____. The _____ _____ are:

1.) _____

2.) _____

3.) _____

and the _____ section to CLIMBING THE LADDER TO LEADERSHIP is _____. A good leader has to be _____ at _____ to _____ to strive to be _____ _____ to his or her _____. One must _____ a _____ of _____, _____, and continue to be _____ about his or her _____ in their organization.

Notice, in regards to (Diagram 4 page 74); the third section along with the three characteristics mentioned are at the top of the Pyramid. Remember the old saying,

"_____ _____ _____ and _____ its _____ down. Leader – ship is _____ _____ - as well as_____, _____ and _____ _____ to act – for certain shared goals that _____ the _____ - the _____ and _____, the _____ and _____ - of _____ and the people they _____. (Martin Luther King, Jr. On leadership Inspiring & Wisdom For Challenging Times; Donald T. Phillips, p.23)

<u>Webster's Definition:</u>

Motivation - the reason or reasons one has for acting or behaving in a particular way; the greater desire or willingness of someone to do something.

79

Through _____, _____, and _____; _____ _____ will _____ by _____ _____ _____ _____ within his or her organization. They are the following four:

1.) _____
2.) _____ an _____ of _____ _____
3.) _____ a _____ of _____
4.) _____ a _____ _____ _____

These four benefits are _____ for any good leadership to _____ _____ _____ to his or her _____ with their organization. This will _____ _____ to _____ _____ _____ and _____ within the organization. The _____ is for leadership to _____ through _____, _____, being _____ and _____ through _____! Good leaders and leadership _____ to _____ with that goal within his or her organization.

80

A good leader know that he or she _____ _____, so he or she on a _____ _____ _____ _____ to _____ the _____ within others. This third section, and three characteristics are the _____ to _____ these four ways to _____ _____ within others in the organization. One must have a _____ _____ of _____ _____ within!

"In creating and gaining widespread acceptance of a nation, leaders provide the only effective mechanism that can truly overcome the natural human tendency to resist change." (Martin Luther King, Jr. On leadership Inspiring & Wisdom for Challenging Times; Donald T. Phillips, p.316)

You can't get people to respond to anything if they aren't stimulated." (Martin Luther King, Jr. On leadership Inspiring & Wisdom for Challenging Times; Donald T. Phillips, p.330)

Peter M. Senge once said, "The most effective people are those who can hold their vision while remaining committed seeing current reality clearly." (The Fifth Discipline: The Art & Practice of the Learning Organization)

Turn your attention to the scriptures for reference.

Scriptures:

Galatians 2:20 – I am crucified with Christ: nevertheless I live; yet not I, but Christ liveth in me: and the life which I now live in the flesh I live by the faith of the Son of God, who loved me, and gave himself for me.

Matthew 16:24-26 – Then said Jesus unto his disciples, if any man will come after me, let him deny himself, and take up his cross, and follow me.

For whosoever will save his life shall lose it: and whosoever will lose his life for my sake shall find it.

For what is a man profited, if he shall gain the whole world, and lose his own soul? Or what shall a man give in exchange for his soul?

2 Timothy 1:13 – Hold fast the form of sound words, which thou hast heard of me, in faith and love which is in Christ Jesus.

Deuteronomy 34:10 – And there arose not a prophet since in Israel like unto Moses, whom the LORD knew face to face,

Psalms 116:12 – What shall I render unto the LORD for all his benefits toward me?

Write down how you plan to be totally committed to your cause in ministry and as a leader.

_____

_____

_____

_____

_____

A good leader _____ that _____ _____ is _____ _____; but for it to be _____ _____; it must _____ _____ ___ _____ and _____ _____; which are, first; the two sections: _____ and _____. Now the six _____ are the following: _____, _____, _____, _____, _____, and _____. When it comes to any type(s) of disputes within an organization, good leadership _____ _____ it with _____ and _____ , having _____, _____, _____, with the _____ of others within the organization. They may even have to _____ with much _____ to the _____ of someone to _____. A good leader also _____ that _____ can _____ ____ _____ with the organization. Sometimes _____ is _____.

At this time, let us draw our attention to (Diagram 4 page 76)
[Open Discussion – 15 Minutes]

At this time, we want to define the two sections.

Webster's Definition:

Assurance – a positive declaration to give confidence; a promise; confidence or certainty of one's abilities.

Ensurance – cause (a product or idea) to be or become obsolete by replacing it with something new; the act or means of ensuring; specifically: insurance; make certain of obtaining or providing

How would you handle: DISPUTING THE STATUS QUO IS ESSENTIAL FOR CHANGE?

_____
_____
_____
_____
_____

A good leader of a leadership's _____, in part is to _____, _____, and _____ _____ _____ within his or her organization.

"Your organization will prosper or die as a result of your ability to create, embody, and communicate a vision." (Martin Luther King, Jr. On leadership Inspiring & Wisdom For Challenging Times; Donald T. Phillips, p.330)

_____, a good leader will _____ him or herself _____ the other _____ to remain _____.

"In general leaders are in the business of working with people – working with them, interacting with them, achieving results in the best interests of the majority or the group at large." (Martin Luther King, Jr. On leadership Inspiring & Wisdom for Challenging Times; Donald T. Phillips, p.286)

"Remember that the guardians of the status quo will lash out against the person or organization that they consider most responsible for the emergence of the new order." (Martin Luther King, Jr. On leadership Inspiring & Wisdom for Challenging Times; Donald T. Phillips, p.274)

Great leaders are _____ _____ about his or her people's _____ to _____ _____ and _____ and the _____ of their people's _____ _____ with the _____ _____ and _____ that are _____ _____. Sometimes leadership _____ a _____ _____ of _____ within his or her organization because _____.

Some _____ their _____ to the _____ causing a _____ _____ within the organization. A good leader must _____ by _____ in the _____; that says, "_____ is _____ _____. A good leader is _____ _____ and _____ _____ _____ _____ within his or her organization.

Why is this, a key factor to leadership?

"Achieving results is directly proportional to your willingness and ability to interact with people." (Martin Luther King, Jr. On leadership Inspiring & Wisdom for Challenging Times; Donald T. Phillips, p.228)

88

In other words: the more _____ the _____ _____, the more _____ that will be _____. There are ____ _____ why any good leader _____ to _____ the _____ of _____ the _____ of others within his or her organization. They are the following:

1.) Have a _____ to _____ for ____ _____
2.) Have _____ in _____ your _____ _____
3.) _____ _____ _____ learning through_____ _____
4.) _____ the _____ of _____
5.) _____ to the _____ and _____ of others
6.) Have a _____ for _____ and _____ _____

Now these (6) strategies must _____ _____ sections two and four of CLIMBING THE LADDER TO LEADERSHIP; which are: _____ and _____.

89

Below are a few scriptures for references.

Scriptures:
1 Corinthians 7:17-24 – But as God hath distributed to every man, as the LORD hath called every one, so let him walk. And so ordain I in all churches.

Is any man called being circumcised? Let him not become uncircumcised. Is any called in uncircumcision? Let him not be circumcised.

Circumcision is nothing, and uncircumcision is nothing, but the keeping of the commandments of God.

Let every man abide in the same calling wherin he was called. Art thou called being a servant? Care not for it: but if thou mayest be made free, use it rather.

For he that is called in the Lord, being a servant, is the Lord's freeman: likewise also he that is called, being free, is Christ's servant. Ye are bought with a price; be not ye the servants of men. Brethren, let every man. Wherin he is called, therein abide with God.

2 Peter 3:9 – The Lord is not slack concerning his promise, as men count slackness; but is longsuffering to us-ward, not willing that any should perish, but that all should come to repentance.

John 5:18 – Therefore the Jews sought the more to kill him, because he not only had broken the Sabbath, but said also that God was his Father, making himself equal with God.

"Effective visions provide context, give purpose, and establish meaning." (Martin Luther King, Jr. On leadership Inspiring & Wisdom for Challenging Times; Donald T. Phillips, p.316)

A good leader _____ his or her _____ _____ _____.
He or she _____ to _____ the _____ by doing the following steps:

    1.) _____ the _____.
    2.) _____ _____ with _____.
    3.) _____ on _____, _____, and _____.

Any _____ _____ has an _____ that this can be _____ _____ _____. In other words, there will be much _____ for a good leader to _____ and _____. For a good leader to _____, it must be done with _____ _____ and being very _____.

One must _____ _____ the _____ through the following _____ _____:

    1.) _____   7.) _____

    2.) _____   8.) _____

    3.) _____   9.) _____

    4.) _____   10.) _____

    5.) _____   11.) _____

    6.) _____

and the following _____ _____:

    1.) _____

    2.) _____

    3.) _____

All ___ _____ must be in _____ _____ _____ a good leader's organization; for it to _____ _____ and _____ within the _____ of the _____.

Webster's Definition:

Preparation – the action or process of making ready or being made ready for use or consideration; something done to get ready for an event or undertaking.

Longevity – long life; long existence or service.

Decisive – setting an issue; producing a definite result; (of a person) having or showing the ability to make decisions quickly and effectively.

This will _____ _____ _____ of _____, _____, and _____ within the _____ and _____. That is; _____ through _____ and one being _____. Being able to _____ _____, _____, and etc. on a _____ _____ with _____ _____ is _____ to _____ others _____ within a good leader's organization. A good leader always has a _____ of _____ and _____ their _____ over a _____ _____ because there may be a need for _____.

How do you see these (11) characteristics interacting with preparation, being decisive, and longevity; to execute, have …. then communicate it and do it within an organization and leadership?

_____

_____

_____

_____

_____

A good leader will _____ calm in _____ of _____.

_____, _____, _____, _____, _____, and _____ are _____ _____ to getting anything done within an organization during this _____ of _____ something _____ and _____.

"When making a decision, understand the facts, consider various solutions and their consequences, make sure that the decision is consistent with your objections, and effectively communicate and implement it." (Martin Luther King, Jr. On leadership Inspiring & Wisdom For Challenging Times; Donald T. Phillips, p.193)

This is a _____ of _____ then _____ and next _____ at its _____. Remember a good leader _____ _____ _____ _____ _____ within his or her organization. _____ is _____ for the _____ of any organization and leadership. A good leader is always _____ to _____ that _____ his or her _____ within the organization.

Consider the follow scriptures below.

Scriptures:
Ephesians 1:10 – That in the dispensation of the fullness of times he might gather together in one all things in Christ, both which are in heaven, and which are on earth; even in him:

Hebrews 9:17-18 – For a testament is of force after men are dead: otherwise it is of no strength at all while the testator liveth. Whereupon neither the first testament was dedicated without blood.

James 2:17 – Even so faith, if it hath not works, is dead being alone.

Philippians 4:9 – Those things, which ye have both learned, and received, and heard, and seen in me, do: and the God of peace shall be with you.

Hebrews 11:1-2 – Now faith is the substance of things hope for, the evidence of things not seen.

For by it the elders obtained a good report.

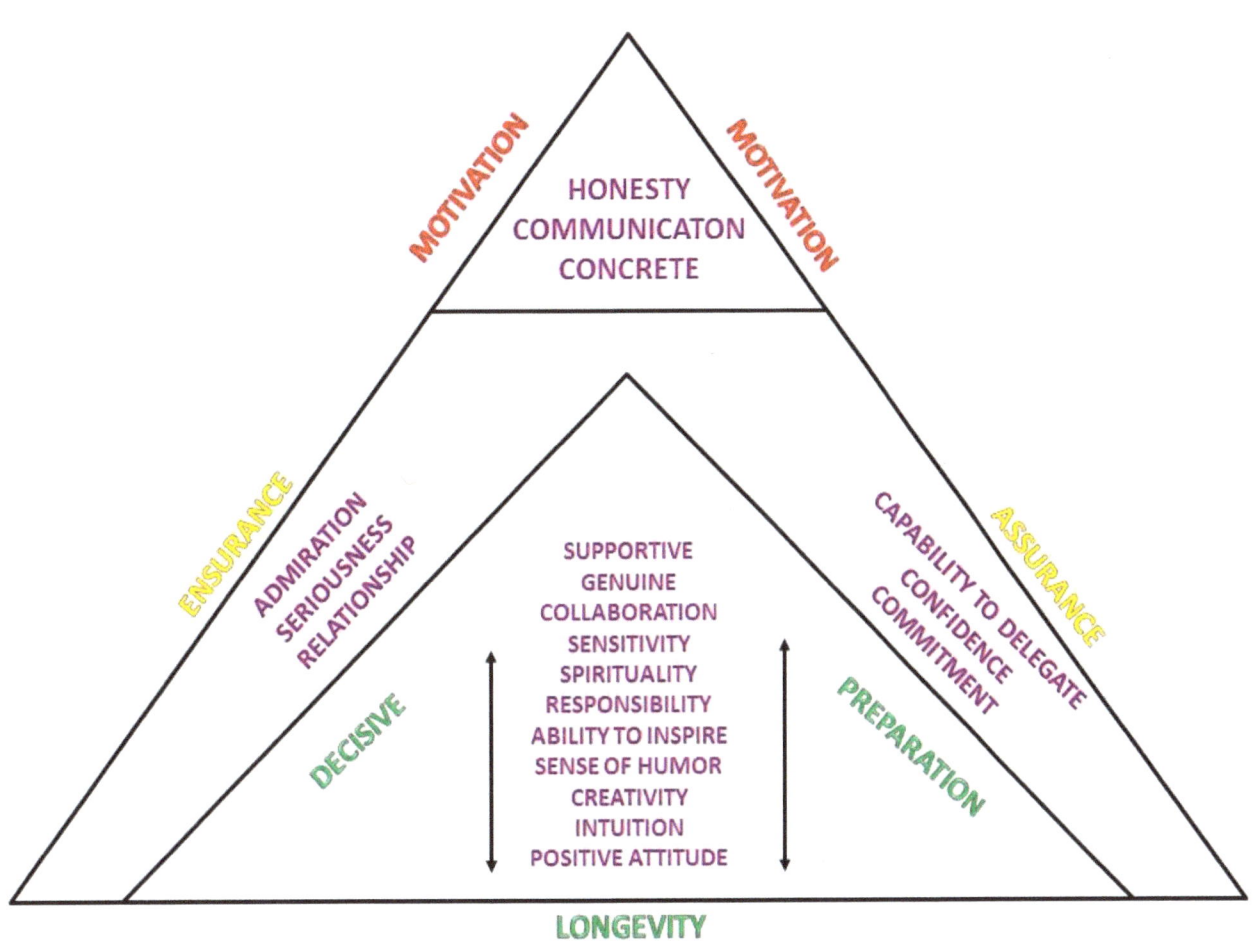

Diagram 5

Now let's look at some exercises, where one will have to decide on what characteristics and sections to implement for each scenario that is given.

Exercise 1

Mrs. Sue Annie Mae Johnson is the Senior Secretary for "Longtime Enterprises" in Raleigh, NC. She has been with the company for 35 years. She is now 58 years old. Mrs. Johnson, at several different times, has been very forgetful. Mrs. Johnson's forgetfulness has been very costly to the company. Last week, Mrs. Johnson was supposed to send off 10 contracts for the company to receive $50,000 in contributions for its business endeavors. Longtime Enterprises has been around for 80 years and has a great reputation. Longtime Enterprises motto is "Think long and stay strong!" Mrs. Johnson forgot to mail off the contracts after they were diligently prepared. Mrs. Johnson forgot and they were on her desk in her mail tray, as the deadline passed. Mr. Richard Max, the Vice-President of Longtime Enterprises calls down from New York to check on the status of the 10 contracts and finds out that they never made it to the Post Office because Mrs. Johnson forgot.

Mr. Max is livid because this isn't the first time Mrs. Johnson forgot to do something that severely cost Longtime Enterprises a great lost. There have been a total of 15 different times Longtime Enterprises took a financial hit because of Mrs. Johnson. Mr. Max pulled up the data on Longtime Enterprises and records showed the company lost a quarter of a million dollars. Mr. Max calls down from corporate and informs leadership that something has to be done for these loses. Longtime Enterprises leadership has called for a meeting to discuss the matter.

You are part of the leadership team. How would you handle this situation? Which of the 6 sections and which of the 20 characteristics would you implement to resolve this situation with Mrs. Johnson? (Write down your answer)

_____

_____

_____

_____

_____

_____

_____

Exercise 2

Mr. Blue Downs is a deacon at Narrow Road Missionary Baptist Church. Deacon Downs has been a deacon at the church for over 40 years. The church just celebrated its 70th church anniversary in 2016. Deacon Downs grew up in the church; he has been a member all 66 years of his life. This past Sunday, Deacon Downs needed help in paying his light bill the next day. Deacon Downs is also on the Board of Trustees and is the one that makes the church deposits every week. On Monday morning while on his way to the bank, Deacon Downs goes into the money bag and takes out $200 so he can pay his light bill.

Deacon Downs didn't think anything about it because his money will go into his account tonight, so he said he will just go back down to the bank, fill out a deposit slip and put the $200 into the church account. Nobody will ever know, Deacon Downs thought to himself and the Lord. Deacon Downs forgot to fill out another bank slip after he took out the $200 from the money bag and he just handed the money bag to the teller at the window. The teller noticed the larger amount difference from the bank slip and called the Pastor.

You are the Pastor, how would you handle this situation; which of the 6 sections and which of the 20 characteristics would you implement to resolve this situation with Deacon Downs? (Write down your answer)

_____

_____

_____

_____

_____

_____

_____

Looking at Diagram 5 on page 98, create you a diagram for each Exercise 1 & 2; showing the sections you selected grouped with the characteristics that relate.

FINAL EXAM
(Open Book)

Multiple Choice

1.) The definition of a Leader is.

  a. something that led
  b. a person who directs a force or unit
  c. a person who has commanding authority of force
  d. a person or performer of a principal group

Fill in the Blank

2.) What are the (6) sections of Climbing the Ladder to Leadership.

    1.) _____   4.) _____

    2.) _____   5.) _____

    3.) _____   6.) _____

True or False

3.) The tallest ladder in the world is 120'-0" tall with 135 rungs. T or F (Circle One)

Fill In The Blank

4.) The one major benefit for any individual who desires to become a leader is _____.

True or False

5.) People tend to sacrifice more when there's a clear channel of working together with leadership. T or F (Circle One)

Fill In The Blank

6.) When _____ a good leader must _____ the presence of a quality of _____ with calm dignity and wise _____ _____.

Multiple Choice

7.) A good leader must have a heart of _____.

  a. gratitude
  b. being a servant
  c. servitude
  d. none of the above

True or False

8.) Having confidence can be a very instrumental access in a leader's life. T or F (Circle One)

Answer the Question

9.) What is definitely a test by itself? _____

10.) Write the scripture Deuteronomy 13:4.

_____

_____

_____

True or False

11.) A good leader with a positive attitude will develop a strong appreciation within his or her organization. T or F (Circle One)

Fill In The Blank

12.) A good leader must spend _____ _____ observing _____.

Multiple Choice

13.) Proverbs 2:6 – Out of his _____ cometh knowledge and understanding.

a.) heart
b.) mind
c.) mouth
d.) none of the above

Answer the Question

14.) What characteristic does a good leader need to be walking in for the sake of others? _____

True or False

15.) As people began to derive inspiration from their involvement, I realized that the cause leaves your own hands.
T or F (Circle One)

16.) Responsibility – the fact of a duty to deal with something having the state of control over someone. T or F (Circle One)

17.) When a good leader makes up in his or her mind of taking responsibility he or she is prepared to do something that serves the cause. T or F (Circle One)

Answer the Question

18.) A good leader, on a daily basis, will always strive to do the following what?

_____

_____

_____

_____

Fill In The Blank

19.) Hope _____ and _____ a good leader and it causes other to _____ within the organization.

True or False

20.) A good leader must be militant as well as moderate. T or F (Circle One)

Answer the question

21.) What did J. Paul Getty say?

_____
_____
_____
_____

22.) A good leader strives to always do what?

_____

_____

_____

_____

True or False

23.) A good leader who is genuine always measures his or her words by their deeds and it will be heard. T or F (Circle One)

Answer the Question

24.) Which characteristic leads to the building of enthusiasm?

_____

25.) What are the three things that having a strong supportive structure within a organization does?

1.) _____

3.) _____

2.) _____

Answer the Question

26.) What is the seventeenth characteristic?

_____

Multiple Choice

27.) A good leader _____ his or her organization with people of strong character.

a. establishes
b. builds
c. looks to builds
d. none of the above

True or False

28.) Proverbs 13:20 – He that walketh with men shall be wise but a companion of being a fool shall be destroyed.

T or F (Circle One)

Fill In The Blank

29.) A good leader is constantly furthering his or her _____ to strengthen their leadership.

Answer the Question

30.) What is the sole purpose concept of the characteristic; admiration?

_____
_____
_____
_____

True or False

31.) Admiration within a leadership will lead within the organization a want to be more used. T or F (Circle One)

Answer the Question

32.) What is the first thing that a good leader must start with in Climbing the Ladder to Leadership? _____

True or False

33.) Sometimes leadership can only express their words with concrete action. T or F (Circle One)

Answer the Question

34.) Which section is at the top of the Pyramid to Climb the Ladder to Leadership? _____

35.) What are the four major benefits that good leadership is led by?

a.) _____

b.) _____

c.) _____

d.) _____

Fill In The Blank

36.) One must have a _____ of _____ _____.

Answer the Question

37.) What does Psalms 116:2 say?

_____

_____

_____

_____

_____

True or False

38.) Assurance – a positive declaration to give certainty; a promise; or certainty of one's abilities. T or F (Circle One)

39.) A good leader of a leader's role, in part, is to only direct and compose the supporting structure within his or her organization. T or F (Circle One)

Answer the Question

40.) What is the "Law of Life? _____

41.) What is the sixth strategy?

_____

_____

42.) A good leader strives to travel the distance by doing what three things?

a.) _____

b.) _____

c.) _____

Fill In The Blank

43.) All _____ must be in full operation throughout a good leader's organization; for it to function properly and professionally within the umbrella of the leadership.

True or False

44.) A good leader is always prepared to do anything that serves his or her cause within the organization. T or F (Circle One)

Fill In The Blank

45.) For a leader to _____, it must be done with _____ _____ and being very decisive.

Answer the Question

46.) Looking at Diagram 5 on page 60: what are the characteristics with Motivation?

_____

_____

47.) On page 46 Diagram 4; what is the list of characteristics with Disputing The Status Quo Essential For Change?

_____

_____

_____

_____

Fill In The Blank

48.) On page 48, what is characteristic number six and what letter does it fall under? _____

49.) On page 44, what are the six names at the top called? _____

50.) What did you learn in this leadership training of "Climbing the Ladder to Leadership?"

_____

_____

_____

_____

_____

_____

Name: _____   Date:_____

Instructor: _____   Final Score: _____

Grade: _____

BIOGRAPHY OF OVERSEER
CLAYTON D. BERRY

Bishop Clayton Deyane Berry was born on December 26, 1971 in Washington, D.C. to Carrie and the late Odis Berry. He is the third of four siblings. He graduated from Northwestern High School in Hyattsville, Maryland. After graduating, he went on to pursue his Architectural Engineering Certification from Maryland Drafting Institute, Langley Park, Maryland. He has a bachelor's degree in Ministry through International Seminary, Plymouth, Florida. He also has a master's degree in Ministry and a doctorate in Ministry both through Andersonville Theological Seminary, Camilla, Georgia. He is the author of two books entitled, "Climbing the Ladder to Leadership (teacher's manual) and "Climbing the Ladder to Leadership (workbook)!"

At the age of 19, Bishop Berry accepted Christ into his life while a member of Trinity Bible Mission Church in Landover, Maryland. His spiritual father and mentor, the late Pastor Robert Fletcher, was a great positive influence on the dedication and commitment that Bishop Berry has for the works of the Lord.

While serving at Trinity, Bishop Berry served in many capacities and was quickly elevated from Sunday School Teacher, to Sunday School Superintendent, to Deacon in training. He was a member of the Male Chorus, where not only did God use his voice, but also his gifts as a percussionist. He was very active in the Youth Department and Drama Ministry. He served in the Usher Ministry, Evangelism Ministry, Transportation Ministry, and the Ministry of Helps.

He was divinely led to Hope Christian Church, under the leadership of Bishop Wayman and Overseer Sandra Kirkman. It wasn't long after becoming part of the Hope Family that God spoke to Bishop Kirkman and told him to elevate then Deacon Berry to the position of Elder. He has worked as the Sunday School Superintendent, percussionist for the Hope Praise Team, Godly Men Ministry, Greeters Ministry, Adjutant to the Bishop, and wherever help is needed.

Through the teaching and Godly guidance at Hope, Bishop Berry was assigned as pastor over the Laurinburg branch of Hope Christian Church from 2008 - 2009. After his assignment there was complete, he was asked to pastor the young adult ministry at the Headquarters church in Fayetteville, North Carolina. On September 9, 2011, Bishop Berry was installed as Pastor of Hope Christian Church Saint Pauls, North Carolina. His faithfulness and commitment to the body led to his elevation to Overseer during the Hope Fellowship International Convocation, October 12, 2015. It was in a dream that God showed him he was going to be elevated to the office of Bishop and shortly thereafter on February 11, 2017, he received a call from Bishop Kirkman confirming what God had showed him, he was elevating him to Bishop. On March 11, 2018, he was consecrated to the office of Bishop.

Bishop Berry reside in Raeford, North Carolina. He currently serves as full time Pastor at Hope Christian Church Saint Pauls, North Carolina. God uses him daily to shine and be a witness to those that he encounters. Bishop Berry performs with the spirit of Job and believes that "Now faith is the substance of things hoped for, the evidence of things not seen. For by it the elders obtained a good report" (Hebrews 11:1-2). He is excited about the promising future that God has for his life.

www.ingramcontent.com/pod-product-compliance
Lightning Source LLC
Chambersburg PA
CBHW041152290426
44108CB00002B/45